# Python Made Simple
# And Practical

© Written By
## James L. Young

The trademarks that are used are without any consent, and the publication of the trademark is without permission or backing by the trademark owner. All trademarks and brands within this book are for clarifying purposes only and are the owned by the owners themselves, not affiliated with this document.

Disclaimer and Terms of Use: The Author and Publisher has strived to be as accurate and complete as possible in the creation of this book, notwithstanding the fact that he does not warrant or represent at any time that the contents within are accurate due to the rapidly changing nature of the Internet. While all attempts have been made to verify information provided in this publication, the Author and Publisher assumes no responsibility for errors, omissions, or contrary interpretation of the subject matter herein.

Any perceived slights of specific persons, peoples, or organizations are unintentional. In practical advice books, like anything else in life, there are no guarantees of results. Readers are cautioned to rely on their own judgment about their individual circumstances and act accordingly.

This book is not intended for use as a source of legal, medical, business, accounting or financial advice. All readers are advised to seek services of competent professionals in the legal, medical, business, accounting, and finance fields.

# Table of Contents

# Introduction

Python is a general-purpose language, which means it can be used to build just about anything, which will be made easy with the right tools/libraries.

Professionally, Python is great for backend web development, data analysis, artificial intelligence, and scientific computing. Many developers have also used Python to build productivity tools, games, and desktop apps, so there are plenty of resources to help you learn how to do those as well.

Python was designed to be easy to understand and fun to use (its name came from Monty Python so a lot of its beginner tutorials reference it). Fun is a great motivator, and since you'll be able to build prototypes and tools quickly with Python, many find coding in Python a satisfying experience. Thus, Python has gained popularity for being a beginner-friendly language, and it has replaced Java as the most popular introductory language at Top U.S. Universities.

Being a very high level language, Python reads like English, which takes a lot of syntax-learning stress off coding beginners. Python handles a lot of complexity for you, so it is very beginner-friendly in that it allows beginners to focus on learning programming concepts and not have to worry about too much details.

As a dynamically typed language, Python is really flexible. This means there are no hard rules on how to build features, and you'll have more flexibility solving problems using different methods (though the Python philosophy encourages using the obvious way to solve things). Furthermore, Python is also more forgiving of errors, so you'll still be able to compile and run your program until you hit the problematic part.

Because Python is a dynamically typed language, the same thing can easily mean something different depending on the context. As a Python app grows larger and more complex, this may get difficult to maintain as errors will become difficult to track down and fix, so it will take experience and insight to know how to design your code or write unit tests to ease maintainability.

As a dynamically typed language, Python is slow because it is too flexible and the machine would need to do a lot of referencing to make sure what the definition of something is, and this slows Python performance down.

At any rate, there are alternatives such as PyPy that are faster implementations of Python. While they might still not be as fast as Java, for example, it certainly improves the speed greatly.

As you step into the programming world, you'll soon understand how vital support is, as the developer community is all about giving and receiving help. The larger a community, the more likely you'd get help and the more people will be building useful tools to ease the process of development.

StackOverflow is a programming Q&A site you will no doubt become intimate with as a coding beginner. Python has 85.9k followers, with over 500k Python questions. Python questions are also the 3rd most likely to be answered when compared to other popular programming languages.

At meetups, you can generally network and learn from fellow developers. Meetups often offer mentorship to those who want it as well. There are 1300+ Python groups on Meetup.com, totaling 608k+ members. Thus, in terms of programming languages, Python is the 3rd largest community.

The more useful projects there are, the more likely someone has already built a function you need and built it well, which will greatly speed up your development process.Over 950 Python projects have over 500 stars.

Python is also known to have an abundance of libraries that assist with data analysis and scientific computing. In addition, PyGames is a neat game engine to build games with if you want to make simple games.

# Python Keywords and Identifier

**Python Keywords**

Keywords are the reserved words in Python.

We cannot use a keyword as variable name, function name or any other identifier. They are used to define the syntax and structure of the Python language.

In Python, keywords are case sensitive.

There are 33 keywords in Python 3.3. This number can vary slightly in course of time.

All the keywords except True, False and None are in lowercase and they must be written as it is. The list of all the keywords are given below.

**Keywords in Python programming language**

| False | class | finally | is | return |
|--------|----------|---------|----------|--------|
| None | continue | for | lambda | try |
| True | def | from | nonlocal | while |
| and | del | global | not | with |
| as | elif | or | yield | |
| assert | else | import | pass | |
| break | except | in | raise | |

Looking at all the keywords at once and trying to figure out what they mean might be overwhelming.

If you want to have an overview, here is the complete list of all the keywords with examples.

**Python Identifiers**

Identifier is the name given to entities like class, functions, variables etc. in Python. It helps differentiating one entity from another.

Rules for writing identifiers

1. Identifiers can be a combination of letters in lowercase (a to z) or uppercase (A to Z) or digits (0 to 9) or an underscore (_). Names like myClass, var_1 and print_this_to_screen, all are valid example.

2. An identifier cannot start with a digit. 1variable is invalid, but variable1 is perfectly fine.

3. Keywords cannot be used as identifiers.

```
>>> global = 1
  File "<interactive input>", line 1
    global = 1
         ^
```

SyntaxError: invalid syntax

4. We cannot use special symbols like !, @, #, $, % etc. in our identifier.

```
>>> a@ = 0
  File "<interactive input>", line 1
```

a@ = 0
∧

SyntaxError: invalid syntax

We cannot use special symbols like !, @, #, $, % etc. in our identifier.

>>> a@ = 0
  File "<interactive input>", line 1
    a@ = 0
    ∧

SyntaxError: invalid syntax

5. Identifier can be of any length.

## Things to care about

Python is a case-sensitive language. This means, Variable and variable are not the same. Always name identifiers that make sense.

While, c = 10 is valid. Writing count = 10 would make more sense and it would be easier to figure out what it does even when you look at your code after a long gap.

Multiple words can be separated using an underscore, this_is_a_long_variable.

We can also use camel-case style of writing, i.e., capitalize every first letter of the word except the initial word without any spaces. For example: camelCaseExample

# Python Objects and Class

In this section, you'll learn about the core functionality of Python, Python objects and classes. You'll learn what a class is, how to create it and use it in your program.

Python is an object oriented programming language. Unlike procedure oriented programming, where the main emphasis is on functions, object oriented programming stress on objects.

Object is simply a collection of data (variables) and methods (functions) that act on those data. And, class is a blueprint for the object.

We can think of class as a sketch (prototype) of a house. It contains all the details about the floors, doors, windows etc. Based on these descriptions we build the house. House is the object.

As, many houses can be made from a description, we can create many objects from a class. An object is also called an instance of a class and the process of creating this object is called instantiation.

## Defining a Class in Python
Like function definitions begin with the keyword def, in Python, we define a class using the keyword class.

The first string is called docstring and has a brief description about the class. Although not mandatory, this is recommended.

Here is a simple class definition.

```
class MyNewClass:
'''This is a docstring. I have created a new class'''
 pass
```

A class creates a new local namespace where all its attributes are defined. Attributes may be data or functions.

There are also special attributes in it that begins with double underscores (__). For example, __doc__ gives us the docstring of that class.

As soon as we define a class, a new class object is created with the same name. This class object allows us to access the different attributes as well as to instantiate new objects of that class.

```
class MyClass:
"This is my second class"
a = 10
def func(self):

print('Hello')
```

```
# Output:
10
print(MyClass.a)
```

```
#       Output:       <function       MyClass.func       at
0x0000000003079BF8>
```

```
print(MyClass.func)
# Output: 'This is my second class'
```

## Creating an Object in Python

We saw that the class object could be used to access different attributes.

It can also be used to create new object instances (instantiation) of that class. The procedure to create an object is similar to a function call.

>>> ob = MyClass()

This will create a new instance object named ob. We can access attributes of objects using the object name prefix.

Attributes may be data or method. Method of an object are corresponding functions of that class. Any function object that is a class attribute defines a method for objects of that class.

This means to say, since MyClass.func is a function object (attribute of class), ob.func will be a method object.

```
class MyClass:
"This is my second class"

a = 10

def func(self):

print('Hello')
```

\# create a new MyClass

ob = MyClass()

\#    Output:    <function    MyClass.func    at 0x000000000335B0D0>

print(MyClass.func)

\#   Output:   <bound   method   MyClass.func   of <\_\_main\_\_.MyClass object at 0x000000000332DEF0>>

print(ob.func)

You may have noticed the self parameter in function definition inside the class but, we called the method simply as ob.func() without any arguments. It still worked.

This is because, whenever an object calls its method, the object itself is passed as the first argument. So, ob.func() translates into MyClass.func(ob).

In general, calling a method with a list of n arguments is equivalent to calling the corresponding function with an argument list that is created by inserting the method's object before the first argument.

For these reasons, the first argument of the function in class must be the object itself. This is conventionally called self.

It can be named otherwise but we highly recommend to follow the convention.

Now you must be familiar with class object, instance object, function object, method object and their differences.

## Constructors in Python

Class functions that begins with double underscore (__) are called special functions as they have special meaning.

Of one particular interest is the __init__() function. This special function gets called whenever a new object of that class is instantiated.

This type of function is also called constructors in Object Oriented Programming (OOP). We normally use it to initialize all the variables.

```python
class ComplexNumber:

    def __init__(self,r = 0,i = 0):

        self.real = r

        self.imag = i

    def getData(self):

        print("{0}+{1}j".format(self.real,self.imag))

# Create a new ComplexNumber object

c1 = ComplexNumber(2,3)

# Call getData() function

# Output: 2+3j

c1.getData()

# Create another ComplexNumber object

# and create a new attribute 'attr'
```

```
c2 = ComplexNumber(5)

c2.attr = 10

# Output: (5, 0, 10)

print((c2.real, c2.imag, c2.attr))

# but c1 object doesn't have attribute 'attr'
# AttributeError: 'ComplexNumber' object has no attribute
'attr'

c1.attr
```

In the above example, we define a new class to represent complex numbers. It has two functions, __init__() to initialize the variables (defaults to zero) and getData() to display the number properly.

An interesting thing to note in the above step is that attributes of an object can be created on the fly. We created a new attribute attr for object c2 and we read it as well. But this did not create that attribute for object c1.

**Deleting Attributes and Objects**
Any attribute of an object can be deleted anytime, using the del statement. Try the following on the Python shell to see the output.

```
>>> c1 = ComplexNumber(2,3)
>>> del c1.imag
>>> c1.getData()
Traceback (most recent call last):
...
AttributeError: 'ComplexNumber' object has no attribute
'imag'
```

```
>>> del ComplexNumber.getData
>>> c1.getData()
Traceback (most recent call last):
...
AttributeError: 'ComplexNumber' object has no attribute
'getData'
```

We can even delete the object itself, using the del statement.

```
>>> c1 = ComplexNumber(1,3)
>>> del c1
>>> c1
Traceback (most recent call last):
...
NameError: name 'c1' is not defined
```

Actually, it is more complicated than that. When we do c1 = ComplexNumber(1,3), a new instance object is created in memory and the name c1 binds with it.

On the command del c1, this binding is removed and the name c1 is deleted from the corresponding namespace. The object however continues to exist in memory and if no other name is bound to it, it is later automatically destroyed.

This automatic destruction of unreferenced objects in Python is also called garbage collection.

# File Handling Operations

## File handling

A file is some information or data which stays in the computer storage devices. You already know about different kinds of file , like your music files, video files, text files. Python gives you easy ways to manipulate these files. Generally we divide files in two categories, text file and binary file. Text files are simple text where as the binary files contain binary data

which is only readable by computer.

## File opening

To open a file we use open() function. It requires two arguments, first the file path or file name, second which mode it should open. Modes are like

* "r" -> open read only, you can read the file but can not edit / delete anything inside
* "w" -> open with write power, means if the file exists then delete all content and open it to write
* "a" -> open in append mode

The default mode is read only, ie if you do not provide any mode it will open the file as read only. Let us open a file

```
>>> fobj = open("love.txt")
>>> fobj
```

```
<_io.TextIOWrapper          name='love.txt'          mode='r'
encoding='UTF-8'>
```

Closing a file

After opening a file one should always close the opened file. We use method close() for this.

```
>>> fobj = open("love.txt")
>>> fobj
<_io.TextIOWrapper          name='love.txt'          mode='r'
encoding='UTF-8'>
>>> fobj.close()
```

Important

Always make sure you explicitly close each open file, once its job is done and you have no reason to keep it open. Because - There is an upper limit to the number of files a program can open. If you exceed that limit, there is no reliable way of recovery, so the program could crash. - Each open file consumes some main-memory for the data-structures associated
with it, like file descriptor/handle or file locks etc. So you could essentially end-up wasting lots of memory if you have more files open that are not useful or usable. - Open files always stand a chance of corruption and data loss.

Reading a file

To read the whole file at once use the read() method.

```
>>> fobj = open("sample.txt")
>>> fobj.read()
'I love Python\nPradeepto loves KDE\nSankarshan loves Openoffice\n'
```

If you call read() again it will return empty string as it already read the whole file. readline() can help you to read one line each time from the file.

```
>>> fobj = open("sample.txt")
>>> fobj.readline()
'I love Python\n'
>>> fobj.readline()
'Pradeepto loves KDE\n'
```

To read all the lines in a list we use readlines() method.

```
>>> fobj = open("sample.txt")
>>> fobj.readlines()
['I love Python\n', 'Pradeepto loves KDE\n', 'Sankarshan loves Openoffice\n']
```

You can even loop through the lines in a file object.

```
>>> fobj = open("sample.txt")
>>> for x in f:
...     print(x, end=' ')
```

...
I love Python
Pradeepto loves KDE
Sankarshan loves Openoffice
Let us write a program which will take the file name as the input from the user and show the content of the file in the console.

```
#!/usr/bin/env python3
name = input("Enter the file name: ")
fobj = open(name)
print(fobj.read())
fobj.close()
```

In the last line you can see that we closed the file object with the help of close() method.
The output

```
$ ./showfile.py
Enter the filename: sample.txt
I love Python
Pradeepto loves KDE
Sankarshan loves Openoffice
```

Using the with statement

In real life scenarios we should try to use with statement. It will take care of closing the file for you.

```
>>> with open('setup.py') as fobj:
...     for line in fobj:
...         print line,
...
#!/usr/bin/env python3
"""Factorial project"""
from setuptools import find_packages, setup

setup(name = 'factorial',
    version = '0.1',
    description = "Factorial module.",
    long_description = "A test module for our book.",
    platforms = ["Linux"],
    author="Kushal Das",
    author_email="kushaldas@gmail.com",
    url="http://pymbook.readthedocs.org/en/latest/",
    license = "http://www.gnu.org/copyleft/gpl.html",
    packages=find_packages()
    )
```

Writing in a file

Let us open a file then we will write some random text into
it by using the write() method.

```
>>> fobj = open("ircnicks.txt", 'w')
>>> fobj.write('powerpork\n')
>>> fobj.write('indrag\n')
>>> fobj.write('mishti\n')
>>> fobj.write('sankarshan')
```

```
>>> fobj.close()
```

Now read the file we just created

```
>>> fobj = open('ircnicks.txt')
>>> s = fobj.read()
>>> print(s)
powerpork
indrag
mishti
sankarshan
```

copyfile.py

In this example we will copy a given text file to another file.

```
#!/usr/bin/env python3
import sys
if len(sys.argv) < 3:
    print("Wrong parameter")
    print("./copyfile.py file1 file2")
    sys.exit(1)
f1 = open(sys.argv[1])
s = f1.read()
f1.close()
f2 = open(sys.argv[2], 'w')
f2.write(s)
f2.close()
```

**Note:**

This way of reading file is not always a good idea, a file can be very large to read and fit in the memory. It is always better to read a known size of the file and write that to the new file.

You can see we used a new module here sys. sys.argv contains all command line parameters. Remember cp command in shell, after cp we type first the file to be copied and then the new file name.

The first value in sys.argv is the name of the command itself.

```
#!/usr/bin/env python3
import sys
print("First value", sys.argv[0])
print("All values")
for i, x  in enumerate(sys.argv):
    print(i, x)
```

The output

```
$ ./argvtest.py Hi there
First value ./argvtest.py
All values
0 ./argvtest.py
1 Hi
2 there
```

Here we used a new function enumerate(iterableobject), which returns the index number and the value from the iterable object.

Count spaces, tabs and new lines in a file

Let us try to write an application which will count the spaces, tabs, and lines in any given file.

```python
#!/usr/bin/env python3

import os
import sys

def parse_file(path):
    """
    Parses the text file in the given path and returns space,
tab & new line
    details.

    :arg path: Path of the text file to parse

    :return: A tuple with count of spacaes, tabs and lines.
    """
    fd = open(path)
    i = 0
    spaces = 0
    tabs = 0
    for i,line in enumerate(fd):
```

```python
        spaces += line.count(' ')
        tabs += line.count('\t')
    #Now close the open file
    fd.close()

    #Return the result as a tuple
    return spaces, tabs, i + 1

def main(path):
    """
    Function which prints counts of spaces, tabs and lines in
a file.

    :arg path: Path of the text file to parse
    :return: True if the file exits or False.
    """
    if os.path.exists(path):
        spaces, tabs, lines = parse_file(path)
        print("Spaces %d. tabs %d. lines %d" % (spaces, tabs,
lines))
        return True
    else:
        return False

if __name__ == '__main__':
    if len(sys.argv) > 1:
        main(sys.argv[1])
    else:
        sys.exit(-1)
```

```
sys.exit(0)
```

You can see that we have two functions in the program , main and parse_file where the second one actually parses the file
and returns the result and we print the result in main function. By splitting up the code in smaller units (functions) helps us to organize the codebase and also it will be easier to write test cases for the functions.

Let us write some real code

Do you know how many CPU(s) are there in your processor? or what is the model name? Let us write some code which can help us to know these things.

If you are in Linux, then you can actually view the output of the lscpu command first. You can actually find the information in a file located at /proc/cpuinfo.

Now try to write code which will open the file in read only mode and then read the file line by line and find out the number of CPU(s).

# Python dictionaries

Dictionaries are a data structure in Python that are very similar to associative arrays. They are non-ordered and contain "keys" and "values." Each key is unique and the values can be just about anything, but usually they are string, int, or float, or a list of these things.

Dictionaries are defined with {} curly braces.

Here is the sample code :

'''

One of the most useful data types in python is the python dictionary.

If you are familiar with other languages, think of it like an associative
array.

The idea of the dictionary is to have what are called keys and values. Despitebeing ordered if you print a dictionary out, there is no actual
order to dictionaries.

All keys are unique

So before we used two lists and assumed their association, searched for index, and found information about 1 item in 1 list from another.

Now here, everything is contained in the same location, and makes more sense

Let us show an example:

'''

# Dictionary of names and ages.
exDict = {'Jack':15,'Bob':22,'Alice':12,'Kevin':17}

print(exDict)
How old is Jack?

print(exDict['Jack'])
We find a new person that we want to insert:

exDict['Tim'] = 14
print(exDict)
Tim just had a birthday though!

exDict['Tim'] = 15
print(exDict)
Then Tim died.

```
del exDict['Tim']
print(exDict)
```
Next we want to track hair color

```
exDict = {'Jack':[15,'blonde'],'Bob':[22,
'brown'],'Alice':[12,'black'],'Kevin':[17,'red']}
print(exDict['Jack'][1])
```

# Built in functions

We cover absolute value (abs()), the help() functions, max(), min() ...which are how to find maximum and minimum of a list, how to round a number with round(), as well as ceil() and floor(), even though these last two are NOT built in, it just seemed like a good time to bring them up. Finally, we cover converting floats, ints, and strings to and from each other.

There are still quite a few other built in functions to Python 3, but the others are not really meant for a basics tutorial.

Sample code for the built in functions that are covered in the video:

Absolute Values:

```
 exNum1 = -5
exNum2 = 5
print(abs(exNum1))
if abs(exNum1) == exNum2:
   print('True!')
```
The Help function:

This is probably one of the most under-utilized commands in Python, many people do not even know that it exists. With help(), you can type it with empty parameters to

1

engage in a search, or you can put a specific function in question in the parameter.

```
help()Or...
import time
# will work in a typical installation of Python, but not in
the embedded editor
help(time)Max and Min:
```

How to find the maximum or highest number in a list...

or how to find the lowest or minimum number in a list.

```
exList = [5,2,1,6,7]

largest = max(exList)
print(largest)

smallest = min(exList)
print(smallest)
Rounding:
```

Rounding will round to the nearest whole. There are also ways to round up or round down.

```
x = 5.622
x = round(x)
print(x)

y = 5.256
```

```
y = round(y)
print(y)
```

Converting data types:

Many times, like reading data in from a file, you might find the datatype is incorrect, like when we mean to have integers, but they are currently in string form, or visa versa.

Converting a string to an integer:

```
 intMe = '55'
intMe = int(intMe)
print(intMe)
```

Converting and integer to a string:

```
 stringMe = 55
stringMe = str(stringMe)
print(stringMe)
```

Converting an integer to a float:

```
 floatMe = 55
floatMe = float(floatMe)
print(floatMe)
```

You can also convert floats to strings, strings to floats, and more. Just make sure you do a valid operation. You still cannot convert the letter h to a float.

# OS Module

The main purpose of the OS module is to interact with your operating system. The primary use I find for it is to create folders, remove folders, move folders, and sometimes change the working directory. You can also access the names of files within a file path by doing listdir(). We do not cover that in this video, but that's an option.

The os module is a part of the standard library, or stdlib, within Python 3. This means that it comes with your Python installation, but you still must import it.

Sample code using os:

```
import os
```

All of the following code assumes you have os imported. Because it is not a built-in function, you must always import it. It is a part of the standard library, however, so you will not need to download or install it separately from your Python installation.

```
curDir = os.getcwd()
print(curDir)
```

The above code will get your current working directory, hence "cwd."

To make a new directory:

os.mkdir('newDir')

To change the name of, or rename, a directory:

os.rename('newDir','newDir2')
To remove a directory:

os.rmdir('newDir2')

With the os module, there are of course many more things we can do. In many scenarios, however, the os module is actually becoming outdated, as there is a superior module to get the job done. We will get to those soon enough. It is still a good idea to at least know some of the basics of the os module. I especially like to use it to create directories. If you ever create a setup.py file, the creation of directories and the placing of files within them will be essential.

# SYS module

The sys module allows you to use stdin() and stdout(), as well as stderr(), but, most interestingly, we can utilize sys.argv(). To many, this is a confusing concept, but it is pretty simple and very useful once you learn it. The idea of sys.argv is to allow you to pass arguments through to Python from the command line.

This ability acts as a bridge to the ability to communicate between Python and other languages, which can then communicate back through the shell to interact.

With stdout and stdin, we can pass messages and errors through to the command line, or just use it for logging purposes.

Here is some basic code that matches the video:

```
import sys

sys.stderr.write('This is stderr text\n')
sys.stderr.flush()
sys.stdout.write('This is stdout text\n')
```

Above, we have some of the basic stderr and stdout statements. Try them out in both a shell like bash or cmd.exe, then also try them in your Python shell.

```
def main(arg):
    print(arg)

main(sys.argv[1])
```

This code utilizes argv, which allows you to pass through arguments from the shell to your Python script or program. You will get an error if you run this without some arguments from the shell. You can always put an if-statement that asks whether sys.argv has a length greater than, for example, one, since here, we are looking for at least two.

Keep in mind that the above code is really only able to shine when you open up your command line / bash, run the script with python scriptname.py, and then add commands to it. Naturally, the script's name will be the first in the list of argv, but then anything else passed through after will be subsequent on the list. Definitely a fun tool to use, and a great way to communicate between languages and other programs.

# Python urllib tutorial for Accessing the Internet

The urllib module in Python allows you access websites via your program. This opens up as many doors for your programs as the internet opens up for you. urllib in Python 3 is slightly different than urllib2 in Python 2, but they are mostly the same. Through urllib, you can access websites, download data, parse data, modify your headers, and do any GET and POST requests you might need to do.

Some websites do not appreciate programs accessing their data and placing weight on their servers. When they find out that a program is visiting them, they may sometimes choose to block you out, or serve you different data that a regular user might see. This can be annoying at first, but can be overcome with some simple code. To do this, you just need to modify the user-agent, which is a variable within your header that you send in. Headers are bits of data that you share with servers to let them know a bit about you. This is where Python, by default, tells the website that you are visiting with Python's urllib and your Python version. We can, however, modify this, and act as if we are a lowly Internet Explorer user, a Chrome user, or anything else really!

I would not recommend just blindly doing this, however, if a website is blocking you out. Websites will also employ other tactics as well, but usually they are doing it because they also offer an API that is specifically made more programs to access. Programs are usually just interested in the data, and do not need to be served fancy HTML or CSS data, nor data for advertisements, etc.

Here is the sample code:

Here is the first and easiest example of using urllib. We just need to import urllib.requests. From there, we assign the opening of the url to a variable, where we can finally use a .read() command to read the data. The result is a massive mess, but we did indeed read the source code.

```
#Used to make requests
import urllib.request

x = urllib.request.urlopen('https://www.google.com/')
print(x.read())
```

Soon, we'll be using regular expressions to clean up the result. The problem is web pages use all sorts of HTML, CSS and javascript to make webpages appealing to the eye. Our programs really just don't care what the website looks like. We just want the text usually, so we need to get rid of all of the fluff. To do that, regular expressions become pretty useful, so we'll head there soon, after covering regex.

Next, sometimes, we want to put in values, or GET/POST, from/to a URL. There are two methods of data transfer with urls, and they are GET and POST. The natural method is a GET request, which means you make a request and you get data. The other is POST, where you send data into the server, like you post some data, and you get a request based on the post.

An example:

http://pythonprogramming.net/?s=basics&submit=Search

You see there are 2 variables here. You can see them because of the equals sign. The first variable is denoted with a question mark, and all of the subsequent ones are denoted with the & sign.

There are multiple ways to pass values through like this, you can just hard-code them, or you can use urllib to do it. Let's show an example of requests with urllib:

```
# used to parse values into the url
import urllib.parse
```

```
url = 'https://www.google.com/search'
values = {'q' : 'python programming tutorials'}
```

Above, we're defining the variables that we plan to POST to the url we specify.

From there, below, we're needing to first url encode all of the values. This is basically things like converting "spaces" to %20, for example.

Then we encode to utf-8 bytes. We make our request, adding in one more value, data, which is the encoded dictionary of keys and values, or better understood in this scenario as variables and their values. Then we open the url with the request that we've built, which we call a response, since that's what we get with it. Finally, we read that response with a .read().

```
data = urllib.parse.urlencode(values)
data = data.encode('utf-8') # data should be bytes
req = urllib.request.Request(url, data)
resp = urllib.request.urlopen(req)
respData = resp.read()
```

```
print(respData)
```
Turns out, Google will return a 405, method not allowed. Google is not happy with our request! Try the above on another website, modifying the variables. Find a website with a search bar, and see if you can make use of it via Python.

Finally, header modification. Sometimes, websites do not appreciate being visited by robots, or they might treat them differently. In the past, most websites, if they had a stance at all, would just block programs. Now, the prevailing method seems to be to serve different data to programs, so they don't realize as easily what has happened, or maybe to share information with the developers. Sometimes, they also simply serve the program with limited data, to keep the load on their servers low. Wikipedia used to outright block programs, but now they serve a page, same with Google. This is usually a page that is not what you actually want, so you will need to work around it.

Whenever you visit a link, you send in a header, which is just some basic information about you. This is how Google Analytics knows what browser you are using, for example.

Within the header, there is a value called user-agent, which defines the browser that is accessing the website's server.

If you are using the default python user-agent with urllib, then you are announcing yourself as Python-urllib/3.4, if your Python version is 3.4. This is either foreign to the website, or they will just block it entirely. A work around for this is to just identify yourself as something else entirely.

```
try:
    x                                              =
urllib.request.urlopen('https://www.google.com/search?q=t
est')
    #print(x.read())

    saveFile = open('noheaders.txt','w')
    saveFile.write(str(x.read()))
    saveFile.close()
except Exception as e:
    print(str(e))
```

The above output is from Google, who knows you are Python. Over the years, how Google and other websites have handled programs has changed, so this might change as well in time. The current response they are giving is just a default search page, once you parse through all the mess of code that is returned.

Google is doing this because we're telling Google who we are, a urllib Python bot! Let's change that by modifying our user-agent in the header.

```
try:
    url = 'https://www.google.com/search?q=python'

    # now, with the below headers, we defined ourselves as a simpleton who is
    # still using internet explorer.
    headers = {}
    headers['User-Agent'] = "Mozilla/5.0 (X11; Linux i686) AppleWebKit/537.17 (KHTML, like Gecko) Chrome/24.0.1312.27 Safari/537.17"
    req = urllib.request.Request(url, headers = headers)
    resp = urllib.request.urlopen(req)
    respData = resp.read()

    saveFile = open('withHeaders.txt','w')
    saveFile.write(str(respData))
    saveFile.close()
except Exception as e:
    print(str(e))
```

Above, we do basically the same thing, only this time, we build our request first, passing through the URL and the new modified headers. Then, we make the request and our response is indeed different. We actually get the data we were interested in back!

# Regular Expressions with regex

There are many times where a programmer with want to split or search in a body of text for something. Say you are looking for any prices within a body of text. Basically, you are looking for a dollar sign ($), followed by at least 1 number, maybe a decimal point, and maybe more numbers. Sometimes, there will be a decimal point before any numbers, such as with something under a dollar. Try to think of a way that you'd incorporate the very large number of possibilities, it is pretty hard. This is where regular expressions come in.

Regular expressions are used to sift through text-based data to find things. Regular expressions express a pattern of data that is to be located. Regex is its own language, and is basically the same no matter what programming language you are using with it.

In Python 3, the module to use regular expressions is re, and it must be imported to use regular expressions. Re is a part of the standard library, meaning you will not need to do any downloading and installing to use it, it is already there.

Let me break down how prices would be discovered in a regex frame of mind:

You'd tell the regular expression module that: You are looking for the string to BEGIN with a dollar sign. Then you are either looking a group of digits, or an immediate period / decimal point. From here, you would keep looking for digits, commas, and periods until you finally reach an ending period before a space (indicating the end of a sentence rather than a decimal point), or just a space. This is exactly how you will structure a real regular expression.

Here is a quick cheat sheet for various rules in regular expressions:

Identifiers:

\d = any number
\D = anything but a number
\s = space
\S = anything but a space
\w = any letter
\W = anything but a letter
. = any character, except for a new line
\b = space around whole words
\. = period. must use backslash, because . normally means any character.
Modifiers:

{1,3} = for digits, u expect 1-3 counts of digits, or "places"
+ = match 1 or more
? = match 0 or 1 repetitions.
* = match 0 or MORE repetitions

$ = matches at the end of string

^ = matches start of a string

| = matches either/or. Example x|y = will match either x or y

[] = range, or "variance"

{x} = expect to see this amount of the preceding code.

{x,y} = expect to see this x-y amounts of the precedng code

White Space Charts:

\n = new line

\s = space

\t = tab

\e = escape

\f = form feed

\r = carriage return

Characters to REMEMBER TO ESCAPE IF USED!

. + * ? [ ] $ ^ ( ) { } | \

Brackets:

[] = quant[ia]tative = will find either quantitative, or quantatative.

[a-z] = return any lowercase letter a-z

[1-5a-qA-Z] = return all numbers 1-5, lowercase letters a-q and uppercase A-Z

The code:

So, we have the string we intend to search. We see that we have ages that are integers 2-3 numbers in length. We could also expect digits that are just 1, under 10 years old. We probably wont be seeing any digits that are 4 in length, unless we're talking about biblical times or something.

```
import re
exampleString = '''
Jessica is 15 years old, and Daniel is 27 years old.
Edward is 97 years old, and his grandfather, Oscar, is 102.
'''
```

Now we define the regular expression, using a simple findall method to find all examples of the pattern we specify as the first parameter within the string we specify as the second parameter.

```
ages = re.findall(r'\d{1,3}',exampleString)
names = re.findall(r'[A-Z][a-z]*',exampleString)

print(ages)
print(names)
```

# How to Parse a Website with regex and urllib

When you use Python 3 and urllib to parse a website, you get all of the HTML data, like using "view source" on a web page. This HTML data is great if you are viewing via a browser, but is incredibly messy if you are viewing the raw source. For this reason, we need to build something that can sift through the mess and just pull the article data that we are interested in. There are some web scraping libraries out there, namely BeautifulSoup, which are aimed at doing this same sort of task.

On to the code:

```
import urllib.request
import re

url = 'http://pythonprogramming.net/parse-website-using-regular-expressions-urllib/'

req = urllib.request.Request(url)
resp = urllib.request.urlopen(req)
respData = resp.read()
```

Up to this point, everything should look pretty typical, as you've seen it all before. We specify our url, our values dict, encode the values, build our request, make our request, and then store the request to respData. We can print it out if we want to see what we're working with. If you are using an IDE, sometimes printing out the source code is not the greatest idea. Many webpages, especially larger ones, have very large amounts of code in their source. Printing all of this out can take quite a while in the IDLE. Personally, I prefer to just view-source. In Google Chrome, for example, control+u will view-source.

Alternatively, you should be able to just right-click on the page and select view-source. Once there, you want to look for your "target data." In our case, we just want to take the paragraph text data. If you're looking for something specific, then what I suggest you do is copy some of the "thing" you are looking for. So in the case of specific paragraph text, highlight some of it, copy it, then view the source. Once there, do a find operation, control+f usually will open one up, then paste in what you are looking for. Once you've done that, you should be able to find some identifiers near what you are looking for. In the case of paragraph data, it is paragraph data because people tell the browser it is. This means usually that there are literally paragraph tags around what we want that look like:

<p>text goes here</p>
Some websites get fancy with their HTML and do things like

```
<p class="derp">text here</p>
```

...keep this in mind. With that in mind, most websites just use simple paragraph tags, so let's show that:

```
paragraphs = re.findall(r'<p>(.*?)</p>',str(respData))
```

The above regular expression states: Find me anything that starts with a paragraph tag, then in our parenthesis, we say exactly "what" we're looking for, and that's basically any character, except for a newline, one or more repetitions of that character, and finally there may be 0 or 1 of THIS expression. After that, we have a closing paragraph tag. We find as many of these that exist. This will generate a list, which we can then iterate through with:

```
for eachP in paragraphs:
    print(eachP)
```

# Tkinter intro

The tkinter module is a wrapper around tk, which is a wrapper around tcl, which is what is used to create windows and graphical user interfaces. Here, we show how simple it is to create a very basic window in just 8 lines. We get a window that we can resize, minimize, maximize, and close! The tkinter module's purpose is to generate GUIs. Python is not very popularly used for this purpose, but it is more than capable of doing it.

Let's walk through each step to making a tkinter window:

Simple enough, just import everything from tkinter.

```
from tkinter import *
```
Here, we are creating our class, Window, and inheriting from the Frame class. Frame is a class from the tkinter module. (see Lib/tkinter/__init__)

Then we define the settings upon initialization. This is the master widget.

```
class Window(Frame):

    def __init__(self, master=None):
        Frame.__init__(self, master)
        self.master = master
```

The above is really all we need to do to get a window instance started.

Root window created. Here, that would be the only window, but you can later have windows within windows.

root = Tk()

Then we actually create the instance.
app = Window(root)
Finally, show it and begin the mainloop.

root.mainloop()

# Tkinter buttons

Once you've figured out the basics to a tkinter window, you might fancy the addition of some buttons. Buttons are used for all sorts of things, but generally are great to incite some interaction between the program and the user. Adding buttons is a two-fold thing in the end. In this video, we show just plainly how to add a button. The addition of a button and its button-like functionality is great, but, in the end, we actually want the button to do something. We'll get there, but first let's just show the button.

Here's our new code:

```
from tkinter import *

class Window(Frame):

    def __init__(self, master=None):
        Frame.__init__(self, master)
        self.master = master
        self.init_window()

    #Creation of init_window
    def init_window(self):

        # changing the title of our master widget
        self.master.title("GUI")
```

```
    # allowing the widget to take the full space of the root
window
    self.pack(fill=BOTH, expand=1)

    # creating a button instance
    quitButton = Button(self, text="Quit")

    # placing the button on my window
    quitButton.place(x=0, y=0)

root = Tk()

#size of the window
root.geometry("400x300")

app = Window(root)
root.mainloop()
```

So here we see a few new concepts. The first is self.init_window(). Why have we done this? Well, in the world of window-making, what we might normally refer to as a "window," is actually correctly called a frame. So that outer edge that people generally call a window is actually the frame. In the first tutorial, we actually just created the frame for windows. I know, I know... earth-shattering things coming at you.

So, once you have the frame, you need to specify some rules to the window within it. here, we initialize the actual window, which we can begin to modify. The next major thing we see is the init_window() function in our window class. Here, we give the window a title, which adds the title of GUI. Then we pack, which allows our widget to take the full space of our root window, or frame.

From there, we then create a button instance, with the text on it that says quit. While tkinter is very basic and simplistic, I sometimes fear that its simplicity is very confusing to programmers. At least for me, I wondered, how we actually get "quit" written on the button. Surely it would take a lot of work? What about making the button go up and down like a button? All of this is just plain done for us. So when you say text="quit," that's really all you have to do and tkinter handles all of the rest. Finally, when we're done creating this button instance, we place it on the window. Here, we place it at the coordinates of 0,0. This can also be quite confusing, because 0,0 may make people expect the quit button to be at the lower left. Instead, it appears at the upper-left. When it comes to computer design, like css or here, 0,0 means upper left. Adding to x moves right, as expected. Adding to the y variable, however, moves down, which is contrary to what you're taught in your graphing lessons in school.

# Tkinter event handling

In this scenario, we are adding a quit event to our quit button, which currently does nothing when clicked on. In basically every circumstance, we're going to want to have our buttons actually do something or perform an action rather than just appear there. This is called an event when someone clicks on something, and we can write code to handle events. Generally, we want to write code that is in line what the expectation of the user that created the event. The more in-line your program can be with what the user intends to happen with their events, the more user-friendly it is going to be.

In tkinter, event handling is as simple as adding a command, which we'll make into a function. Even though this function we create is a basic 1-line function that simply calls another function, we can see how we can later create more complex functions for our events.

from tkinter import *

# Here, we are creating our class, Window, and inheriting from the Frame
# class. Frame is a class from the tkinter module. (see Lib/tkinter/__init__)
class Window(Frame):

```python
    # Define settings upon initialization. Here you can specify
    def __init__(self, master=None):

        # parameters that you want to send through the Frame class.
        Frame.__init__(self, master)

        #reference to the master widget, which is the tk window
        self.master = master

        #with that, we want to then run init_window, which doesn't yet exist
        self.init_window()

    #Creation of init_window
    def init_window(self):

        # changing the title of our master widget
        self.master.title("GUI")

        # allowing the widget to take the full space of the root window
        self.pack(fill=BOTH, expand=1)

        # creating a button instance
        quitButton                =                Button(self, text="Exit",command=self.client_exit)
```

```
    # placing the button on my window
    quitButton.place(x=0, y=0)

  def client_exit(self):
    exit()

# root window created. Here, that would be the only window, but
# you can later have windows within windows.
root = Tk()

root.geometry("400x300")

#creation of an instance
app = Window(root)

#mainloop
root.mainloop()
```

# Tkinter menu bar

Now that we've got the basic window, buttons, and event handling down, we're ready to tackle the idea of a menu bar. The way tkinter works, along with quite a few graphics/windows operations work, is with a main window, then you sort of build things on top of it, then display everything all at once, which gives the appearance of a singular package. What makes tkinter most confusing, at least to me, is that you have to work both forwards and backwards in relation to your goal.

So, when I make programs, I usually work backwards from my goal. I know what the end objective is going to be, and then I take steps in reverse, first calling a non-existent function as if it works how I might need it to, then I define it to fit how I need it to act. With tkinter, this methodology is used as well, only you have to do some of the beginning steps, then you have to go to the end and work backwards. Let's hit the code to understand better:

```
# Simple enough, just import everything from tkinter.
from tkinter import *
```

```
# Here, we are creating our class, Window, and inheriting
from the Frame
# class. Frame is a class from the tkinter module. (see
Lib/tkinter/__init__)
```

```python
class Window(Frame):

    # Define settings upon initialization. Here you can specify
    def __init__(self, master=None):

        # parameters that you want to send through the Frame class.
        Frame.__init__(self, master)
        #reference to the master widget, which is the tk window
        self.master = master

        #with that, we want to then run init_window, which doesn't yet exist
        self.init_window()

    #Creation of init_window
    def init_window(self):

        # changing the title of our master widget
        self.master.title("GUI")

        # allowing the widget to take the full space of the root window
        self.pack(fill=BOTH, expand=1)

        # creating a menu instance
        menu = Menu(self.master)
        self.master.config(menu=menu)
```

```
        # create the file object)
        file = Menu(menu)

        # adds a command to the menu option, calling it exit,
and the
        # command it runs on event is client_exit
        file.add_command(label="Exit",
command=self.client_exit)

        #added "file" to our menu
        menu.add_cascade(label="File", menu=file)

        # create the file object)
        edit = Menu(menu)

        # adds a command to the menu option, calling it exit,
and the
        # command it runs on event is client_exit
        edit.add_command(label="Undo")

        #added "file" to our menu
        menu.add_cascade(label="Edit", menu=edit)

    def client_exit(self):
        exit()

# root window created. Here, that would be the only
window, but
# you can later have windows within windows.
```

```
root = Tk()

root.geometry("400x300")

#creation of an instance
app = Window(root)

#mainloop
root.mainloop()
```

Sometimes I like to describe things line by line, and sometimes I think it can make it confusing. For tkinter, you've probably noticed I've been commenting the heck out of it and describing. Hopefully that helps a bit. So, here, we can see that the menus are all done within init_window().

We see to begin, we need a menu instance, then we bind that instance as a menu. Then, we create a menu within the menu. Then, we add the items to the menu within a menu...then we do it again.

...and people are quickly lost with this. It's quite a confusing way to go about it at first, but that's what we've got. Once you get comfortable with tkinter, you can perform these operations much quicker. If you are confused, then I highly suggest you watch the video as well, since I show how the grouping of the 3 lines of object creation, adding options, then appending to the main menu sort of simplifies the process.

# Tkinter images, text, and conclusion

To round off our intro to tkinter, I will be showing how to add text and images to your window. We're going to make them show conditionally, to illustrate how simple it is to make the windows interactive.

```
# Simple enough, just import everything from tkinter.
from tkinter import *

#download and install pillow:
# http://www.lfd.uci.edu/~gohlke/pythonlibs/#pillow
from PIL import Image, ImageTk

# Here, we are creating our class, Window, and inheriting
from the Frame
# class. Frame is a class from the tkinter module. (see
Lib/tkinter/__init__)
class Window(Frame):

    # Define settings upon initialization. Here you can
specify
    def __init__(self, master=None):

        # parameters that you want to send through the Frame
class.
        Frame.__init__(self, master)
```

```
    #reference to the master widget, which is the tk
window
    self.master = master

    #with that, we want to then run init_window, which
doesn't yet exist
    self.init_window()
  #Creation of init_window
  def init_window(self):

    # changing the title of our master widget
    self.master.title("GUI")

    # allowing the widget to take the full space of the root
window
    self.pack(fill=BOTH, expand=1)

    # creating a menu instance
    menu = Menu(self.master)
    self.master.config(menu=menu)

    # create the file object)
    file = Menu(menu)

    # adds a command to the menu option, calling it exit,
and the
    # command it runs on event is client_exit
    file.add_command(label="Exit",
command=self.client_exit)
```

```
    #added "file" to our menu
    menu.add_cascade(label="File", menu=file)

    # create the file object)
    edit = Menu(menu)

    # adds a command to the menu option, calling it exit,
and the
    # command it runs on event is client_exit
    edit.add_command(label="Show  Img",
command=self.showImg)
    edit.add_command(label="Show Text",
command=self.showText)

    #added "file" to our menu
    menu.add_cascade(label="Edit", menu=edit)

  def showImg(self):
    load = Image.open("chat.png")
    render = ImageTk.PhotoImage(load)

    # labels can be text or images
    img = Label(self, image=render)
    img.image = render
    img.place(x=0, y=0)

  def showText(self):
    text = Label(self, text="Hey there good lookin!")
```

```python
        text.pack()

    def client_exit(self):
        exit()


# root window created. Here, that would be the only
window, but
# you can later have windows within windows.
root = Tk()

root.geometry("400x300")

#creation of an instance
app = Window(root)

#mainloop
root.mainloop()
```

# Threading module

Probably one of the largest drawbacks to the Python programming languages is that it is single-threaded. This means that Python will only run on a single thread naturally. If you have a large computational task, you might have already found that it takes Python a very long time to reach a solution, and yet, your processor might sit at 5% usage or even less. There are quite a few solutions to this problem, like threading, multiprocessing, and GPU programming. All of these are possible with Python, and today we will be covering threading. So, what is threading within the frame of Python? Threading is making use of idle processes, to give the appearance of parallel programming. With threading alone in Python, this is not really the case, but we can indeed use threading to make use of idle times and still gain some significant performance increases.

Along with the video above, here is some explained sample code for threading in Python 3:

```
import threading
from queue import Queue
import time
```

So far, we've imported threading, queue and time. Threading is for, well, threading, queue is going to help us make, you guessed it, a queue! Finally, we import time. Our only reason for importing time here is to simulate some idle time with a time.sleep() function.

Next, we're going to define a thread lock. The idea of a threading lock is to prevent simultaneous modification of a variable. So, if two processes begin interaction with a variable with it is, say, 5, and one operation adds 2, and the other adds 3, we're going to end with either 7 or 8 as the variable, rather than having it be 5+2+3, which would be 10. A lock will force an operation to wait until the variable is unlocked in order to access and modify it. Another use for a lock is to aid in input/output. With threading, it becomes quite easy to have two processes modifying the same file, and the data will literally just run over each other. So say you are meaning to save two values, like "Monday" and "Tuesday" to a file, you are intending for the file to just read: "Monday Tuesday," but instead it winds up looking like "MoTunedsadyay." A lock helps this.

print_lock = threading.Lock()

Here, we're looking to use the lock to stop print functions from running over each other in their output.

Now we're ready to create some sort of task to show off threading with:

```python
def exampleJob(worker):
    time.sleep(.5) # pretend to do some work.
    with print_lock:
        print(threading.current_thread().name,worker)
```

So we define this exampleJob function, with a parameter of worker. With that job, we pretend to do something that will cause some idle, and that is just a time.sleep. After that, we use the print lock, which locks while we're doing some output to prevent overlapping. Once the with statement completes, the lock will automatically unlock.

Now we need something that will assign tasks to our threads. Here, we're calling our threads workers.

```python
# The threader thread pulls an worker from the queue and processes it
def threader():
    while True:
        # gets an worker from the queue
        worker = q.get()

        # Run the example job with the avail worker in queue (thread)
        exampleJob(worker)

        # completed with the job
        q.task_done()
```

I'll let the commenting speak for how this one works, as it would be too confusing to split this one up. See the video as well for more explanation if you need it.

Now we've used this "q," but we've not defined it, so we had better do that:

```
# Create the queue and threader
q = Queue()
```

Now let's create our threads, and put them to work!

```
# how many threads are we going to allow for
for x in range(10):
    t = threading.Thread(target=threader)

    # classifying as a daemon, so they will die when the
main dies
    t.daemon = True

    # begins, must come after daemon definition
    t.start()

start = time.time()

# 20 jobs assigned.
for worker in range(20):
    q.put(worker)

# wait until the thread terminates.
```

```
q.join()

# with 10 workers and 20 tasks, with each task being .5
seconds, then the completed job
# is ~1 second using threading. Normally 20 tasks with .5
seconds each would take 10 seconds.
print('Entire job took:',time.time() - start)
```

# CX_Freeze

There may come a time when you've created something very exciting, and you want to share it. Usually, in order to share your Python program, the recipient is going to need to have the same version of Python installed, along with all of the modules used. Well this can be quite tedious to require. The interest in converting to .exe is fairly high for distribution, and there are a couple of options. With Python 2.7, Py2exe is a great choice. For Python 3, I have found cx_freeze to work quite nicely. Here's a tutorial covering how it works.

You'll first need to get cx_Freeze: http://cx-freeze.sourceforge.net/

Once you have cx_freeze, you're ready to get started.

First, you're going to need a python program to convert. For now, stick with standard library modules at most. Here, we'll use the urllib + re tutorial where we parsed Pythonprogramming.net:

```
import urllib.request
import urllib.parse
import re
import time
```

```
url = 'http://pythonprogramming.net'
values = {'s' : 'basics',
       'submit' : 'search'}

data = urllib.parse.urlencode(values)
data = data.encode('utf-8') # data should be bytes
req = urllib.request.Request(url, data)
resp = urllib.request.urlopen(req)
respData = resp.read()

paragraphs = re.findall(r'<p>(.*?)</p>',str(respData))

for eachParagraph in paragraphs:
   print(eachParagraph)

time.sleep(15)
```

We've added a 15 second sleep at the end, so that we can run the executable and see the output before it closes.

I've saved this file as "reandurllib.py."

Now, we create a second file called "setup.py"

```
from cx_Freeze import setup, Executable

setup(name = "reandurllib" ,
    version = "0.1" ,
```

```
    description = "" ,
    executables = [Executable("reandurllib.py")])
```

So, here we're importing from cx_Freeze setup and executable, then we call the setup function, adding 4 parameters. For name, this is the name we want our executable to be. Version is just a version number to give it, description if you want, then finally what shall we convert, using the executable function and the python script's path to be converted as the parameter.

Next, we open up cmd.exe, or bash, or whatever shell we have, navigate to the directory that has the setup.py and the script to be converted, and we run:

python setup.py build

Now we're given a build directory. Within it, we find another directory, and within THAT, we find our executable! If you did everything right, it should parse the search result of basic from PythonProgramming.net, and display the text results for 15 seconds before closing. Awesome, right?

Some things wont be so simple. Converting things like Pygame and Matplotlib are very difficult and are solved in a case-by-case basis. Most things, however, are done very simply like this.

# The Subprocess Module

So this tutorial is a lot more than just the sample code. While you probably can just get by with the others without watching the video, this one is going to probably make no sense without the video. That said:

```
# This tutorial is best followed in a shell / command prompt.
# Open yours up, type python, or python3, and then follow.
import subprocess

# Say you are on windows:
# module  call command in the shell
# you can change that if you'd like, eventually.
# IF YOU ARE NOT IN A SHELL, YOU WILL SEE NO OUTPUT!
subprocess.call('dir', shell=True)
subprocess.call('echo dir', shell=True)
```

So what we're able to do here is communicate to the shell commands from our Python script. The reason this matters is for the same reason that we can communicate from the shell to Python. We can communicate from the shell to Python as we saw earlier, and now we see we can communicate from Python to the shell.
What makes this special, is when you realize that you can do this same thing with other languages as well. So, you

can use, say, java to communicate with the shell, which then passes vars through to a python script, which then communicates back to the shell, which then goes back into the java program... or any program. You can achieve similar results with sockets as well, and it will come down to performance and preference which you choose. I find this method to be far easier, but sometimes more clumsy.

# Matplotlib Crash Course

One of the most popular uses for Python is data analysis. Naturally, data scientists want a way to visualize their data. Either they are wanting to see it for themselves to get a better grasp of the data, or they want to display the data to convey their results to someone. With Matplotlib, arguably the most popular graphing and data visualization module for Python, this is very simplistic to do. In this tutorial, I will be covering all of what I consider to be the basic necessities for Matplotlib. If you are interested in learning more about Matplotlib, then I highly suggest you visit my extensive and dedicated tutorial series on just Matplotlib.

In order to get the Matplotlib, you should first head to Matplotlib.org and download the version that matches your version of Python. From there, it'd be wise to go ahead and make sure you have pyparsing, dateutil, six, numpy, and maybe some of the others mentioned in the video. You can get all of these as well, if you are on a Windows machine by heading to:
http://www.lfd.uci.edu/~gohlke/pythonlibs/#matplotlib

Once you have Matplotlib installed, be sure to open up a terminal or a script, type:

import matplotlib

Make sure there are no errors on the import. If there are, read the error. Most often, either the bit version does not match (64 bit vs 32 bit), or you are missing a package like dateutil or pyparsing.

Once you can successfully import matplotlib, then you are ready to continue.
Here's some basic code to generating one of the most simple graphs that we can, it will take us only 3 lines.

```
#Importing pyplot
from matplotlib import pyplot as plt

#Plotting to our canvas
plt.plot([1,2,3],[4,5,1])

#Showing what we plotted
plt.show()
```

Resulting graph:

adding labels and title to our matplotlib graph
As you progress with Matplotlib, it might be useful to understand how it works fundamentally. This process is true with a lot of computer graphics processes. First, you have some data, then you "draw" that data to a canvas of some sort, but it is only in the computer's memory. Once you've drawn that data, you can then "show" that data. This is so the computer can first draw everything, and then

perform the more laborious task of showing it on the screen.

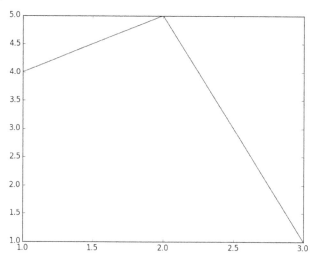

So, with the code above, we just import pyplot from matplotlib, we use pyplot to "plot" some data to the canvas in memory, then we use plt, which is pyplot, to show what we've got.

Now, of course, there are some problems with our graph. First off, we learned in school that we're supposed to put labels on each axis and that we need a title to our graph or chart. Next, in terms of programming, it is unlikely that you will actually be filling in data to the plt.plot() function. Instead, you will, or at least you should, be only passing variables into it. Like plt.plot(x,y). So now let us show plotting variables as well as adding some descriptive labels and a good title!

```
from matplotlib import pyplot as plt

x = [5,8,10]
y = [12,16,6]

plt.plot(x,y)

plt.title('Epic Info')
plt.ylabel('Y axis')
plt.xlabel('X axis')

plt.show()
```

Our new graph:

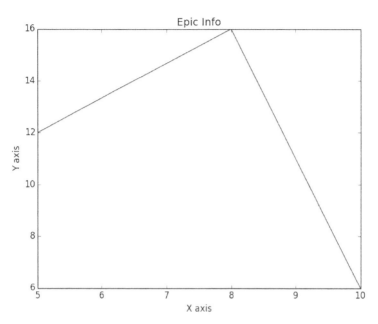

Adding labels and title to our matplotlib graph
Great, now we have titles and labels, and we can see how easily we can plot variables.

Next up, however, our graph is, well, ugly. If you want to learn all of the ins and outs to heavily customizing your graphs, then you will definitely want to check out the Matplotlib series referenced above. Here, my goal is to get you on your way as quick as possible with the basics. Making graphs look decent, however, is definitely important. With this in mind, I have decided to just share matplotlib styles with you. Styles work with matplotlib very much in the same way that CSS stylesheets work with HTML. You can just "import" a stylesheet and use all of the pre-set customizations of that stylesheet. This way, you can save them, and not need to code any style customizations yourself. Eventually, Styles will be built into your matplotlib installation. At the time of my writing this, they are not. This means we'll need to just do it ourselves, luckily, this is relatively easy.

To get styles, head to: pythonprogramming.net/downloads/style.zip

Then, extract that, and move the styles folder within it to c:/python34/matplotlib, where python34 is your python version. If you are not on windows, just make sure the styles folder is in the root matplotlib package folder.

With that, we're ready to use styles. Be sure to poke around the styles files, to get a feel for how they work and maybe customize them yourself a bit if you like. From there, using them is simple enough:

```
from matplotlib import pyplot as plt
from matplotlib import style

style.use('ggplot')

x = [5,8,10]
y = [12,16,6]

x2 = [6,9,11]
y2 = [6,15,7]
# can plot specifically, after just showing the defaults:
```

```
plt.plot(x,y,linewidth=5)
plt.plot(x2,y2,linewidth=5)

plt.title('Epic Info')
plt.ylabel('Y axis')
plt.xlabel('X axis')

plt.show()
```

Here, as you can see, the only reference to styling that we've made is the style.use() function, as well as the line width changes. We could also change the line colors if we wanted, instead of using the default colors, and get a chart like:

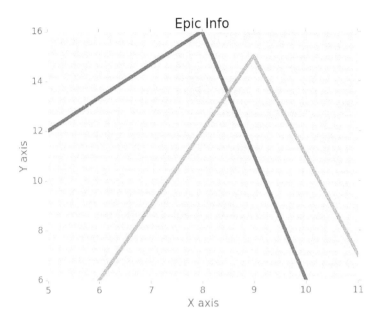

## matplotlib customization

I find it best to go ahead and import styles right away, then make any minor changes that I might want to make later in the script. If you call styles right at the end, you will wind up overwriting any customizing changes that you already made.

Now that we've got this, what more can we do? Well an obvious "basic" thing is legends. Let's add a legend to our chart, and, since it is simple enough, let's learn about grid lines too:

from matplotlib import pyplot as plt

from matplotlib import style

style.use('ggplot')

```
x = [5,8,10]
y = [12,16,6]

x2 = [6,9,11]
y2 = [6,15,7]
```

Up to this, everything is about the same, but now you can see we've added another parameter to our plt.plot(), which is "label." Just to clarify, for those who are not yet totally comfortable with the notion of default parameters in functions, some people may be curious about why we are able to plot the x, y, and color variable without any sort of assignment, but then we have to assign label and linewidth. The main reason here is because there are many parameters to pyplot.plot(). It is really easy to forget their order. X, y, and color is fairly easy to remember the order, people are good at remembering orders of three. After that, the chances of forgetting the proper order get quite high, so it just makes sense. There are also many parameters to edit, so we just call them specifically. Anyway, we can see here that we added a "label," so matplotlib knows what to call the line. This doesn't quite yet give us a legend, however. We need to call plt.legend(). It's important to call legend AFTER you've plotted what you want to be included in the legend.

```
plt.plot(x,y,'g',label='line one', linewidth=5)
plt.plot(x2,y2,'c',label='line two',linewidth=5)
plt.title('Epic Info')
```

```
plt.ylabel('Y axis')
plt.xlabel('X axis')

plt.legend()

plt.grid(True,color='k')

plt.show()
```
legends and gridlines with matplotlib tutorial

Okay, well that's good enough for linear charts I'd say. Keep in mind what I was saying about how matplotlib first "draws" things to a canvas, then finally shows it. Things like legends are drawn when you call them, so, if you are using, say, subplots, and call legends at the very end, only the 2nd subplot would have a legend. If you wanted a legend on each subplot, then you would need to call it per subplot. This is the same with titles! But hey, I didn't even cover subplots (multiple graphs on the same "figure," which just means the same window)... if you are curious about those, check out the in-depth Matplotlib tutorial series, or the specific matplotlib subplots tutorial.

On to bar charts and scatter plots!

Bar charts with matplotlib are basically 1 slight change, same with scatter plots. The only major change I like to make to bar charts is to center them, and that's about it:

```
from matplotlib import pyplot as plt
```

```
from matplotlib import style

style.use('ggplot')

x = [5,8,10]
y = [12,16,6]

x2 = [6,9,11]
y2 = [6,15,7]

plt.bar(x, y, align='center')

plt.bar(x2, y2, color='g', align='center')
plt.title('Epic Info')
plt.ylabel('Y axis')
plt.xlabel('X axis')
plt.show()
```

Result:

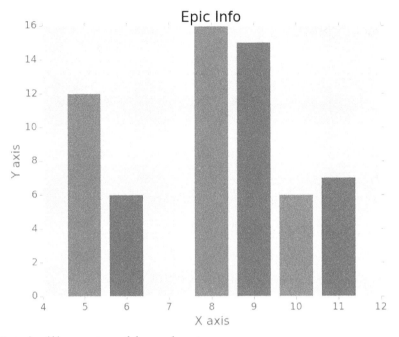

Matplotlib centered bar chart

So, here, we can see instead of plt.plot(), we've used plt.bar(). We also used a new parameter called align, and made it align centered. I like that, you don't have to use it if you don't of course.

How about scatter plots? Super easy, we'll just change .bar() to .scatter(), and remove our align parameter:

from matplotlib import pyplot as plt
from matplotlib import style

style.use('ggplot')
x = [5,8,10]

```
y = [12,16,6]

x2 = [6,9,11]
y2 = [6,15,7]
plt.scatter(x, y)#, align='center')

plt.scatter(x2, y2, color='g')#, align='center')

plt.title('Epic Info')
plt.ylabel('Y axis')
plt.xlabel('X axis')

plt.show()
```

## The result:

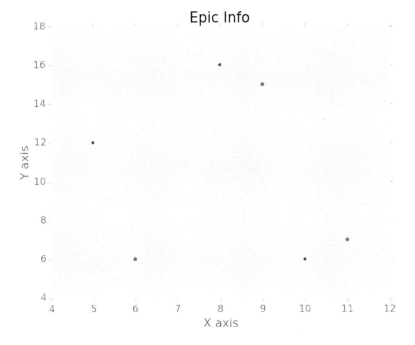

**matplotlib graphing tutorial series**

Great, so we're Matplotlib wizards now, and we're ready to journey into the real world and plot stuff! One of the more popular file types that you'll first start using is CSVs. Eventually, you'll probably find that people stop using CSV files and use either databases or they are using something like HDF5 formatting. For now, let's just cover CSV. There are obviously many ways to read files in Python. You can use Python's CSV module that is a part of the standard library. You can make use of Numpy's loadtxt as well, which we'll be using. Another fantastic choice is using Pandas! So there are many choices to consider, but, for now, we're going to use Numpy. Depending on your goals and requirements, you might eventually wind up choosing something else. I like NumPy because it's very open-ended for data analysis, yet still very powerful. I also think Pandas is going to be a great choice for most people, but it is less open-ended. Enough on that though. Make sure you have NumPy installed. If you do not:

https://pypi.python.org/pypi/numpy
or

http://www.lfd.uci.edu/~gohlke/pythonlibs/#numpy
Once you have NumPy, you're going to need some sample data! Either grab some that you'd like to use if you think you are going to be able to make the necessary edits, or feel free to use this sample data:

Saved as "exampleFile.csv" in the root directory (the same directory) as your current script:

```
1,5
2,7
3,8
4,3
5,5
6,6
7,3
8,7
9,2
10,12
11,5
12,7
13,2
14,6
15,9
16,2
```

Save that, and then the code to plot from this data set:

```
from matplotlib import pyplot as plt
from matplotlib import style
import numpy as np

style.use('ggplot')

x,y = np.loadtxt('exampleFile.csv',
```

```
          unpack=True,
          delimiter = ',')

plt.plot(x,y)

plt.title('Epic Info')
plt.ylabel('Y axis')
plt.xlabel('X axis')

plt.show()
```

Result:

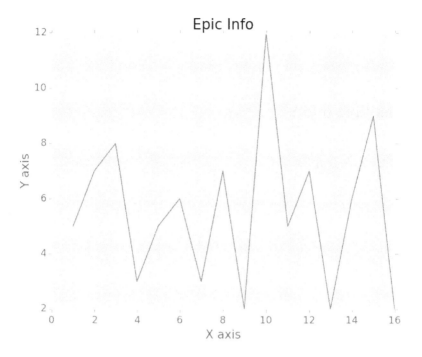

How to graph from CSV files with Matplotlib and NumPy

Here, our major new things are importing numpy, and then using numpy's loadtxt function. Loadtxt can be used to load more than just .txt files. It's just load things with text, that's all. Here, we are unpacking the contents of exampleFile.csv, using the delimiter of a comma. It's important to note here that you MUST unpack the exact same number of columns that will come from the delimiter that you state. If not, you'll get an error.

# Python ftplib

In this section, we cover how to do FTP (file transfer protocol) transfers with ftplib. We'll cover both uploading and downloading files with a remote server.

To start:

```
from ftplib import FTP

#domain name or server ip:
ftp = FTP('123.server.ip')
ftp.login(user='username', passwd = 'password')
```

The above will connect you to your remote server. You can then change into a specific directory with:

```
ftp.cwd('/whyfix/')
```

Now, let's show how we might download a file:

```
def grabFile():

    filename = 'example.txt'

    localfile = open(filename, 'wb')
    ftp.retrbinary('RETR ' + filename, localfile.write, 1024)

    ftp.quit()
    localfile.close()
```

So there are a few things here, so let's walk through it. First, we assign the file name to a variable. Then, we prepare our local file to be written in accordance with whatever the remote file contains.

Next, we retrieve the binary data from the remote server, then we write to the local file what we find. The last parameter there, the 1024, is in reference to buffering. Basically, how much data at a time will we do? So at 1024, 1024 byte chunks will be transferred at a time until the full operation is complete.

Next, how about uploading a file?

```
def placeFile():

    filename = 'exampleFile.txt'
    ftp.storbinary('STOR '+filename, open(filename, 'rb'))
    ftp.quit()

placeFile()
```

About the same here, we take file name and assign it to a variable, then we store the binary data to the filename, with the read data from the file name locally.

Sockets with Python Intro

Sockets are used in networking. The idea of a socket is to aid in the communication between two entities. When you view a website, you are opening a port and connecting to that website via sockets. In this, you are the client, and the website is the server. Quite literally, you are served data.

What are Ports and what are Sockets?

A natural point of confusion here is the difference between sockets and ports. You can think of a port much like a shipping port, where boats dock at the port and unload goods. Then, you can think of the ship itself as the socket. The ocean is the internet. Much like shipping ports, a socket (our ship in this metaphor), is bound by a specific port. Docking at a different port is not allowed, for ships or sockets!

Now, let's go ahead and play with ports and sockets in Python! This can be a slightly confusing topic, so I will do my best to document everything. The video should help as well if you are finding yourself confused.

```
import socket

s          =          socket.socket(socket.AF_INET,
socket.SOCK_STREAM)
print(s)
```

So, we must import socket to use it. This is an included module with your Python 3 distribution

Next, "s" here is being returned a "socket descriptor" by socket.socket. We then print "s" to show what this looks like.

Generally, we use sockets to communicate between a couple of places, so let's show an example of that. One of the most common transmissions of data is between a "client" and "server," most often in the case of a user visiting a website and being served web-content, much like you are being served this page right now. Sockets did that for you.

server = 'pythonprogramming.net'

port = 80

server_ip = socket.gethostbyname(server)
print(server_ip)

Just about any public website will have port 80 open, which is for HTTP access. Most websites will have port 22 open, which is for SSH (secure shell), and many will have 20 and 21 open, which are used for FTP (File Transfer Protocol).

Here is some more information on open ports and hacking:
Open Ports and Hacking

Do open ports mean you are going to be hacked?

It is a common misconception, perpetuated by the media, that an "open port" is all one needs to "hack" a something. The truth is, all websites have open ports, but each port is expecting a specific socket (ship in our metaphor from before), and that specific socket's type of payload of data (ship's cargo) is also known and expected before-hand.

Thus, in our metaphor, if we have a ship that is supposed to be bringing 50 crates full of coffee, but has instead brought over 50 crates of swordfish, immediate red flags are thrown. The same is true with sockets and ports. The socket / ship can be denied.

Then how do hackers get in?

The way sockets and ports are abused by hackers is by taking advantage of vulnerabilities in the programs that have opened specific ports. Every program that uses the internet to provide you a service uses ports, and opens them to the world. Take Skype for example. Skype uses ports 80 and 443. You already know what port 80 is for. 443 is for other types of connections besides port 80's HTTP connections. Via port 443, Skype is expecting a certain type of data, but maybe their security is not perfect, and people are able to use port 443 maliciously because Skype's protocol is not perfectly secure.

Thus, what hackers tend to do, is scan open ports. From the open ports, many times, they can deduce what programs you are running, and proceed to try various attacks against that program's vulnerabilities, especially the historical ones that are generally made public. This is why it is important to keep your software up to date. Most software updates contain security upgrades, fixes, or patches. Even if not specifically explained, the very act of patching an area of code can alert someone that there was something weak there before.

So, above, we were able to access PythonProgramming.net via port 80. From there, we were able to determine the server's IP address by using gethostbyname().

Now, let's make a request, making sure it is in-line with what the port will find acceptable from our socket:

```
request = "GET / HTTP/1.1\nHost: "+server+"\n\n"
s           =          socket.socket(socket.AF_INET,
socket.SOCK_STREAM)
s.connect(("pythonprogramming.net", 80))
```

Above, we defined our request as an HTTP request, where we wanted to "GET" data from the "Host" of PythonProgramming.net

Next, we defined our socket in the same manner as we had before.

Finally, we make our connection to PythonProgramming.net on port 80. This is just a connection. We have defined out request, but not actually made any request, so let's make the request:

```
s.send(request.encode())
result = s.recv(4096)

print(result)
```

First we're sending the request, and encoding it.

Then we're using s.recv to receive the resulting data. The 4096 is a buffer for the data, so that you receive the data in manageable chunks rather than all at once. Finally, we're just printing the result (Though it should be noted this is printing only the first part of the buffer, so the buffer in this case is almost a waste.)

With Python 3, one of the major changes from Python 2 was the differing treatment of strings and bytes. If you want to make a request that is a string, you need to encode it. You will also need to decode any return that you wish to treat like a string. You should just get into the habit mentally that everything you send out over the internet needs to be encoded, and all that you receive needs a

.decode, every time! Python 2 implicitly handled this for us. Python 3 requires us to be explicit, which is more Pythonic anyways.

One of the main pillars of Python is that "explicit is better than implicit. If you have not yet, open a console, and do the following import:

import this

Since I said the buffer was almost a waste, I should probably show how to make the output actually buffer as well. Here's how:

Instead of using print(result), comment or delete that, then do:

```
while (len(result) > 0):
    print(result)
    result = s.recv(4096)
```

# Simple Port Scanner with Sockets

Now that we understand sockets, let's build a simple port-scanner. The idea of a port scanner is to run through a list of ports, testing to see if they are open. We can do this because the steps for using sockets for sending data is first you make the connection, then you try to off-load the request. Re-visiting our ship metaphor, the dock has no idea what contents are in the ship. Thus, if the port is open, the ship can at least dock before anyone knows whether or not what the ship is carrying is supposed to be there.

With our port scanner, we just attempt to dock at various ports, and do nothing else. If we're permitted to dock / connect to open ports, then we know at least the port is open. This is a form of "reconnaissance" for hackers and penetration testers.

```
import socket

s              =              socket.socket(socket.AF_INET,
socket.SOCK_STREAM)

target = input('What website to scan?: ')
```

Here is code you should recognize up to this point. For the target, you could enter website that allows you to do this.

Check out "https://www.hackthissite.org/", or you can always target your own servers.

## WARNING/DISCLAIMER:

It should be noted that port scanning can be seen as, or construed as, a crime. You should never execute a port scanner against any website or IP address without explicit, written, permission from the owner of the server or computer that you are targeting. Port scanning is akin to going to someones house and checking out all of their doors and windows. There is really only reason why anyone would do this, and it is to assess securities and vulnerabilities. Thus, if you have no good reason to be testing these things, it can be assumed you are a criminal.

Also, I have been locked out of my own servers before for running various penetration tests, which was part of the test. A lot of servers have security software that identifies and protects against things like port scans, slowing them down or just outright denying any further connections from the source IP address. Thus, you might find yourself unable to access a server after running a test. For this reason, you may want to use "https://www.hackthissite.org/" instead of just any random site, or even your own.

```
def pscan(port):
   try:
      con = s.connect((target,port))
      return True
   except:
      return False
```

```
for x in range(25):
    if pscan(x):
        print('Port',x,'is open')
```

That's all, for a simple port scanner. What we've done above is simply attempt a connection to a port. If that is successful, our function returns a True, otherwise a False. If True is returned, then our little program will print out the successful port to the console.

# Threaded Port Scanner

As I imagine you discovered, port scanning can be brutally slow, yet, in most cases, is not processing intensive. Thus, we can use threading to drastically improve our speed. There are thousands of possible ports. If it is taking 5-15 seconds per port to scan, then you might have a long wait ahead of you without the use of threading.

Threading can be a complex topic, but it can be broken down and conceptualized as a methodology where we can tell the computer to do another task if the processor is experiencing idle time. In the case of port scanning, we're spending a lot of time just waiting on the response from the server. While we're waiting, why not do something else? That's what threading is for. If you want to learn more about threading, I have a threading tutorial here.

So now we mesh the threading tutorial code with our port scanning code:

```
import threading
from queue import Queue
import time
import socket


# a print_lock is what is used to prevent "double"
modification of shared variables.
# this is used so while one thread is using a variable, others
cannot access
# it. Once done, the thread releases the print_lock.
# to use it, you want to specify a print_lock per thing you
wish to print_lock.
print_lock = threading.Lock()

target = 'hackthissite.org'
#ip = socket.gethostbyname(target)



def portscan(port):
    s          =          socket.socket(socket.AF_INET,
socket.SOCK_STREAM)
    try:
        con = s.connect((target,port))
        with print_lock:
            print('port',port)
        con.close()
```

```
    except:
        pass

# The threader thread pulls an worker from the queue and
processes it
def threader():
    while True:
        # gets an worker from the queue
        worker = q.get()

        # Run the example job with the avail worker in queue
(thread)
        portscan(worker)

        # completed with the job
        q.task_done()

# Create the queue and threader
q = Queue()

# how many threads are we going to allow for
for x in range(30):
    t = threading.Thread(target=threader)

    # classifying as a daemon, so they will die when the
main dies
    t.daemon = True

    # begins, must come after daemon definition
```

```
    t.start()


start = time.time()

# 100 jobs assigned.
for worker in range(1,100):
    q.put(worker)

# wait until the thread terminates.
q.join()
```

# Binding and Listening with Sockets

Up until this point, I have shown you how you can use the socket module to make use of socket connections permitted by other clients and programs. Now it is time to cover how to do this ourselves!

The way this is done should sound fairly expectable, as you know the requirements of sockets. First you bind a socket, then you listen on a port for incoming connections.

```
import socket
import sys

HOST = "
PORT = 5555

s = socket.socket(socket.AF_INET, socket.SOCK_STREAM)
```

Socket import for sockets, sys import to execute a quit if there is a failure.

Next, we specify our host and port. You don't really need the host to be specified, but it is good practice to include it in your code, so we have. Finally, we're specifying a port. Pick whatever you want, just choose a high number so it hopefully doesn't conflict with another program of yours.

```
try:
  s.bind((HOST, PORT))
```

```
except socket.error as msg:
  print('Bind failed. Error Code : ' + str(msg[0]) + '
Message ' + msg[1])
  sys.exit()
```

```
print('Socket bind complete')
```

Here, we are simply attempeting to bind a socket locally, on port 5555. If that fails, then we post the error and exit the program.

```
s.listen(10)
```

```
conn, addr = s.accept()
```

```
print('Connected with ' + addr[0] + ':' + str(addr[1]))
```

Next, we're going to use s.listen to listen. Here, the "10" stands for how many incoming connections we're willing to queue before denying any more.

Now you can run your script. Once you've done that, you should be able to make a connection. You will likely get a security notifcation that you must accept in order to continue with the tutorial. You are getting this notification because the program is trying to open and listen for incoming connections on your behalf. As you might imagine, people might attempt to give you malicious software to do just this.

Accept the warning if you get one, and now you should be able to telnet localhost on the port you chose, which was 5555 for me. So, opening bash, a shell, or cmd.exe, type:

telnet localhost 5555

For now, nothing much will happen, but you should see a black window and your running python script should update with the incoming connection address.

I hope you enjoyed the tutorials.

© James L. Young